Facing Mighty Fears
About Being Apart From Parents

Dr. Dawn's Mini Books About Mighty Fears
By Dawn Huebner, PhD
Illustrated by Liza Stevens
Helping children ages 6–10 live happier lives

Facing Mighty Fears
About Animals
ISBN 978 1 78775 946 6
eISBN 978 1 78775 947 3

Facing Mighty Fears About
Baddies and Villains
ISBN 978 1 83997 462 5
eISBN 978 1 83997 463 2

Facing Mighty Fears
About Health
ISBN 978 1 78775 928 2
eISBN 978 1 78775 927 5

Facing Mighty Fears
About Throwing Up
ISBN 978 1 78775 925 1
eISBN 978 1 78775 926 8

Facing Mighty Fears
About Trying New Things
ISBN 978 1 78775 950 3
eISBN 978 1 78775 951 0

Facing Mighty Fears
About Making Mistakes
ISBN 978 1 83997 466 3
eISBN 978 1 83997 467 0

Facing Mighty Fears About Being Apart From Parents

Dawn Huebner, PhD

Illustrated by Liza Stevens

Jessica Kingsley Publishers
London and Philadelphia

First published in Great Britain in 2024 by Jessica Kingsley Publishers
An imprint of John Murray Press

1

Copyright © Dawn Huebner, PhD 2024
Illustrations copyright © Liza Stevens 2024

A CIP catalogue record for this title is available from the British Library and the Library of Congress

ISBN 978 1 83997 464 9
eISBN 978 1 83997 465 6

Printed and bound in Great Britain by TJ Books Limited

Jessica Kingsley Publishers' policy is to use papers that are natural, renewable, and recyclable products and made from wood grown in sustainable forests. The logging and manufacturing processes are expected to conform to the environmental regulations of the country of origin.

Jessica Kingsley Publishers
Carmelite House
50 Victoria Embankment
London EC4Y 0DZ

www.jkp.com

John Murray Press
Part of Hodder & Stoughton Ltd
An Hachette Company

Grown-ups:

Need ideas about how to use this book?

Please see Dr. Dawn's
Note to Parents and Caregivers
on page 67.

You'll also find a **Resource Section**
highlighting books, websites, and organizations
for parents of anxious kids.

What do baby flamingos, foxes, ferrets, and finches have in common?

They have parents who protect them.

Other animals do, too.

From armadillos to zebras, animal parents go to great lengths to keep their babies safe.

FUN FACT
Male sandgrouse use their feathers to soak up water to feed their thirsty chicks. When the chicks are done sucking from his feathers, the father takes a dust bath since the smell of wet feathers is tempting to prey.

FUN FACT
Strawberry-dart frogs separate their babies to keep them safe. If tadpoles were left together, they'd eat each other.

Why is that?

Do armadillos and zebras love their children as much as your parents love you?

FUN FACT
Baby koalas immediately climb into their mother's pouches when they are born.

FUN FACT
Koalas eat only eucalyptus leaves, which are poisonous. To build their tolerance, mother koalas feed their joeys feces (poop), which is full of digested leaves. After 6 months of eating poop, koalas are able to digest the actual leaves on their own.

FUN FACT
Koalas leave their mothers when they are 1 year old, and set off to find their own territory.

We're not sure if animals feel emotions like love.

What we do know is that they are wired for survival.

In the animal kingdom, that means two things:

→ Staying safe, so you can stay alive.

→ Having as many babies as possible, and keeping your babies safe, so there are animals just like you swimming, flying, and roaming the earth long after you are gone.

FUN FACT
Sows (female pigs) sing their piglets to sleep.

The survival instinct prompts animals to protect their young.

Some go to great lengths to do this, hiding their babies in their mouths, or tucking them into built-in pouches.

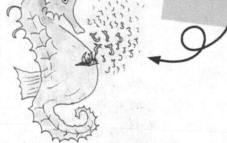

Others sit on their young, or keep them perched on their back or belly.

But baby animals grow. They can't stay in their parents' mouths or pouches forever.

Instead, they start venturing out on their own.

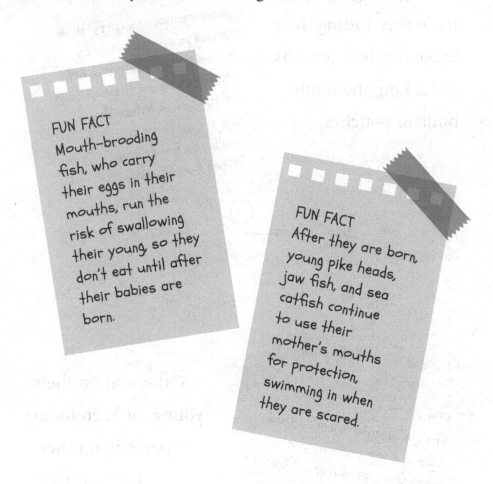

FUN FACT
Mouth-brooding fish, who carry their eggs in their mouths, run the risk of swallowing their young, so they don't eat until after their babies are born.

FUN FACT
After they are born, young pike heads, jaw fish, and sea catfish continue to use their mother's mouths for protection, swimming in when they are scared.

Venturing out is both exciting and scary. The world can be a dangerous place for fox kits, flaminglets, armadillo pups, and zebra foals.

So, as they leave the nest, or the den, or wherever they've been staying, baby animals need to learn new skills.

FUN FACT
Baby pandas are tiny —and blind—at birth. Their mothers cradle them almost constantly for the first few months.

FUN FACT
Baby pandas have a huge growth spurt at age 1, and by 18 months, they have learned everything they need to know to survive on their own.

Animal parents teach their young how to
find food,
stay clean,
remain hidden when sleeping,
and watch out for predators.

It's a lot to learn.

FUN FACT
Baby orangutans stay in physical
contact with their mothers,
clinging to their backs or bellies
for the first 4 months of life.

FUN FACT
By age 6,
orangutans know
what to eat and
where to find
it, and how to
climb trees, build
sleeping nests, and
swing through the
canopy.

For some animals, learning survival skills happens quickly.

Seal pups leave home when they are just 2 weeks old.

Penguin chicks leave at 6 months.

FUN FACT
Father emperor penguins protect eggs while mothers go off to look for food.

FUN FACT
After penguin chicks are born, mothers return to feed them, regurgitating (throwing up) pre-chewed fish into their mouths.

FUN FACT
Male emperor penguins continue to protect their chicks, huddling together in large colonies to keep them warm.

Sometimes it takes longer.

Baby dolphins swim away when they are 6.

FUN FACT
Mother dolphins stay awake for an entire month after each baby is born. Baby dolphins don't sleep, so the mothers must stay awake to keep them safe. Eventually, baby dolphins learn to sleep. Phew!

Male African elephants leave starting at age 9.

FUN FACT
Baby elephants sometimes suck their trunks, like human infants suck their thumbs.

FUN FACT
Baby elephants don't know how to use their trunks when they are born. They blow a lot of bubbles learning how to drink.

FUN FACT
Young female elephants are recruited as babysitters to give mama elephants a break, and to teach the females parenting skills.

Human children take the longest of all, often living at home for 18 or 19 years.

Of course, human parents don't keep their children in pouches, at least not for 18 years.

And they don't keep them in constant sight.
Starting at a young age, most parents encourage
their children to begin doing things on their own.

For some children, the move toward independence
happens smoothly.

For others, the process is bumpy.

Some children worry about doing things on their
own, preferring to stay close to a parent.

But staying with a parent isn't always possible.

There are things children want and need to do that are meant for children alone.

And things parents want and need to do that are meant for grown-ups alone.

So, being apart happens.

FUN FACT
Harp seals take care of their young for 2 weeks, then leave them alone on the ice. The pups survive on fat reserves as they gradually learn to eat crustaceans and small fish.

FUN FACT
Mother gazelles keep a close eye on their young. As they grow, groups of males go off on their own, no longer needing a parent to follow them around.

Spending time apart from parents is important,

and necessary,

and **fun**!

There's a whole wide world waiting to be explored.

But some children find it scary to walk around their own house alone, and can't even imagine exploring the wider world.

To these children, venturing out feels risky.

They worry about getting lost or left behind.

They imagine needing a parent, and not being able to get to them right away.

When they think about being apart, these children get flooded with thoughts of all the horrible things that might happen.

Thinking about all that might go wrong leads to a bunch of nervous questions:

And when there is any choice at all, children who feel nervous about being apart try to stay with their parents all the time.

It just feels safer that way.

Why is that?

Why is separating from parents easy for some children and hard for others?

FUN FACT
During the first 8 years of life, mother chimpanzees teach their young the skills they need to survive, including how to get along with other chimps.

FUN FACT
When young chimpanzees get too aggressive, their mothers scold them with sounds and gestures. Getting along with others is an important part of survival.

The answer has to do with survival, and a part of your brain called the **amygdala** (a-mig-da-la).

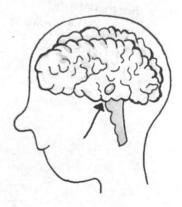

Just like other animals, humans are wired for survival. Not the "have as many babies as possible" part, but the part about staying alive.

To stay alive, we need to stay safe. And to stay safe, we need to know when we are in danger.

That's where the amygdala comes in.

Its job is to alert you to danger.

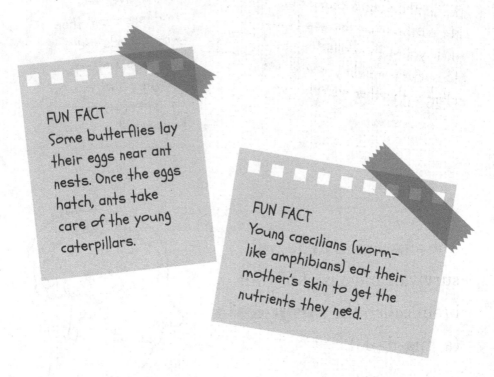

FUN FACT
Some butterflies lay their eggs near ant nests. Once the eggs hatch, ants take care of the young caterpillars.

FUN FACT
Young caecilians (worm-like amphibians) eat their mother's skin to get the nutrients they need.

The amygdala always errs on the side of caution.

It lets you know about things that **might** be problematic, picking up on even the possibility of a bad thing happening.

And then—DANGER! DANGER! DANGER!—the amygdala sounds its alarm.

Amygdala alarms happen inside your head. No one else can hear them.

In fact, even you can't hear them. At least not with your ears.

But you can feel amygdala alarms because they make your heart **pound** and your stomach **churn**. They make you feel like something is very, very wrong.

So, you get scared. As you should.

Feeling scared means your amygdala is doing exactly what it's supposed to do.

There's just one small problem.

Your amygdala isn't always right.

It pulls the alarm when something seems dangerous. But **seeming** dangerous is different from **being** dangerous.

We all have false alarms.

Feeling nervous about being apart from a parent is an example of a false alarm.

Your amygdala gets concerned that something **might** be wrong. So, it warns you, just in case.

But when you go to a different part of your house, or to school, or an activity meant for children, the chance of something major going wrong is tiny.

Your amygdala is making a mistake. You are not in danger.

It's hard to know when your amygdala is making a mistake. Fear always feels like the real thing. It makes you feel like you need to **do** something, to protect yourself so you can stay safe.

FUN FACT
Cheetahs move their young every 4 days to prevent the build-up of smells that might attract predators.

FUN FACT
When they are 18 months old, cheetah cubs leave home. They band together with their siblings for another 6 months before venturing out on their own.

Protecting yourself is the right thing to do when danger is real. But when your amygdala has made a mistake, protecting yourself causes problems. That's because you and your amygdala communicate back and forth.

Your amygdala signals you.

amygdala ⟶ **you**

You respond, which gives your amygdala information about whether the danger is real.

amygdala ⟵ **you**

When you insist on staying with a parent, you are teaching your amygdala that staying together is necessary.

Your amygdala can't help but notice.

Without realizing it, you've taught your amygdala the wrong thing. You have strengthened your own fear.

What a tangle!

You need to let your amygdala know it's safe to do things without your parents, but it doesn't **feel** safe.

How can you fix that?

How can you show yourself AND your amygdala
that being apart is both safe and manageable?

The following three steps can help.

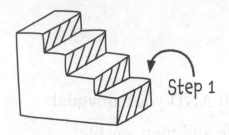

Step 1

1. Quiet your brain.

When your amygdala sounds the alarm, it's impossible to think clearly.

It seems like there really is a problem.

After all, your heart is **POUNDING**, and your stomach is **churning**. It sure feels like there's something wrong.

Your brain is on high alert. Its focus is on **danger**, and nothing else matters.

But not being able to think clearly makes it impossible to sort out whether there really is something wrong.

The alarm is clanging too loudly.

You need to quiet all this down. To calm your brain so your amygdala can see that right now, in this moment, you are safe.

The best way to quiet your amygdala is to breathe.

You might be thinking:

But, actually, if you do it right, it does.

The right way to breathe is slowly and deeply. In through your nose and out through your mouth.

It helps to have something to see, or do, or imagine, while you are breathing.

Here are two techniques you can try:

Tracing Finger Breaths

→ Hold one hand up, fingers spread, palm facing out.

→ Using your other hand, slowly trace each finger, starting with your thumb.

→ As you move up the length of each finger, breathe in through your nose.

→ As you move down each finger, breathe out through your mouth.

→ Trace your fingers slowly.

→ Breathe in the whole time your tracing finger is moving up, and out the whole time your finger is moving down.

→ When you get to the bottom of your little finger, switch hands and do the whole thing again.

Glitter Jar

→ Ask a grown-up to help you make a glitter jar.

→ Find a clear plastic jar or bottle. Clean it both inside and out. If there are labels, remove them.

→ Pour in some glue, filling the jar one third of the way.

→ Add a spoonful or more of glitter. You can use all one color or several colors, and all one size glitter or several sizes.

→ Fill the jar almost to the top with warm (but not boiling) water. Leave two finger-widths of air space at the top.

→ Screw on the lid or cap, then shake the jar.

→ Watch how the glitter moves. If it settles to the bottom too quickly, add more glue. If there isn't enough glitter to swirl around in a pleasing way, add more. If you want to change the color of the water, add a few drops of food coloring.

→ When your glitter jar seems right to you, close the lid tightly. A hot glue gun will seal the lid closed.

→ Your glitter jar is now complete.

→ When you are ready to use it, shake the jar vigorously.

→ Breathe slowly and deeply as you watch the glitter settle.

→ If you have used different shapes of glitter, you can choose a single shape to watch until it falls to the bottom. Breathe while you are watching. Then, find another shape and watch that one fall. Keep watching shapes until all the glitter has settled.

→ If you have used a single size and shape of glitter, shake the jar, and breathe while all the glitter settles.

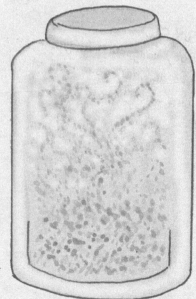

If neither of these techniques feel good to you, work with an adult to find a method that does. Search online for breathing and mindfulness for kids, or check the Resources section at the back of this book.

Once you have found a breathing or mindfulness activity you like, practice it. The more you practice, the better it will work.

FUN FACT
Baby kangaroos (joeys) are as small as a grain of rice when they are born.

FUN FACT
Baby kangaroos stay safe in their mother's pouch for 10 months. After leaving the pouch, they stay close to their mothers for another year, learning how to be independent before venturing out on their own.

Don't wait until you are scared to practice. In fact, it's best to begin when you aren't afraid.

Then, once you've gotten the hang of it, use your special breathing method when you feel scared about doing something on your own.

Breathing won't make your fear disappear, but it will quiet your brain enough to allow you to think more clearly.

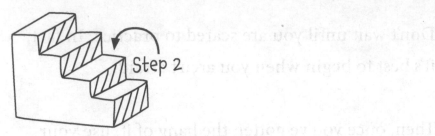

Step 2

2. Do the opposite.

Breathing slowly and deeply will calm your brain enough to get the thinking part working again.

Once you are able to think more clearly, you can remember that this is a false alarm. And that staying with a parent all the time teaches your amygdala the wrong thing.

It strengthens the idea that being apart is dangerous, which means you will keep having these false alarms.

FUN FACT
Baby giraffes take their first steps within an hour of being born.

FUN FACT
Zebra foals become independent from their mothers by age 3.

If you want the false alarms to stop, you need to teach your amygdala that being apart is safe, and that you can handle it.

So, that's what you need to do. The opposite of what you've been doing.

You need to practice being apart.

You might be thinking:

Even *thinking* about separating might cause your amygdala to sound the alarm.

That's why it's important to go slowly.

Just one step at a time.

         staircase.
       climbing a
    like
Almost

Start by thinking about something you *wish* was easier.

Maybe you want to be able to go to your room alone, or to a friend's house.

Maybe you want to sleep in your own bed, or to sign up for an after-school activity that all your friends are doing.

Think of something you need to do, or want to do, but can't, because fear gets in the way.

Then, draw a staircase.

Write the thing you want to be able to do at the top
of the staircase.

Write the opposite of that, the thing you are
currently doing, at the bottom.

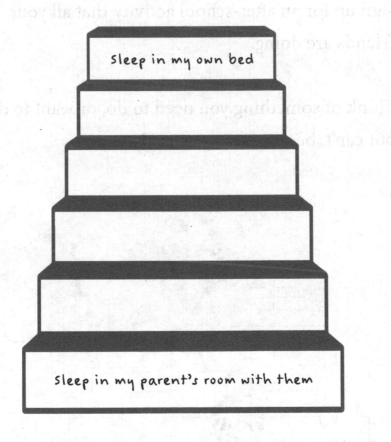

Sleep in my own bed

Sleep in my parent's room with them

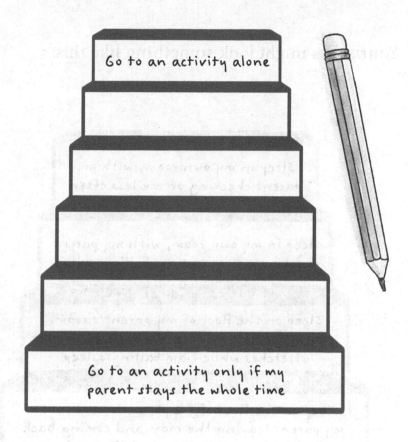

Go to an activity alone

Go to an activity only if my parent stays the whole time

Work with a parent or another adult to fill in the rest of the staircase, starting at the bottom and moving up.

Each step on the staircase should be just a little harder than the one that comes before.

Your stairs might look something like this:

Sleep in my own room, with my parent checking on me less often

Sleep in my own room, with my parent checking on me as I am falling asleep

Sleep on the floor of my parent's room, with my parent leaving the room for longer stretches while I am falling asleep

Sleep on the floor of my parent's room, with my parent leaving the room and coming back to check on me while I am falling asleep

Sleep on the floor of my parent's bedroom. They stay in their own bed while I am falling asleep

Sleep with my parent in their room, in their bed, going to bed at the same time

Or like this:

Walk to my playroom. Sit down. Do something for 15 minutes (not electronics)

Walk to my playroom. Sit down. Draw a picture

Walk to my playroom. Go in. Touch 10 things. Walk back (3 times in a row)

Walk to my playroom alone, then walk back (10 times in a row)

Run to my playroom alone, then run back (10 times in a row)

Go to my playroom (or other room) only with a parent, sibling, or pet

Or like this:

Get dropped off at the activity

Go to the activity while my
parent waits in the car

Go to the activity. My parent
stays for a few minutes, then goes
to a nearby room to wait

Go to the activity with my parent. Every
15 minutes, they step out for a few minutes

Go to the activity with my parent. Every
15 minutes, they step out for a few seconds

Go to an activity only if my parent stays the whole time

Fill in your own staircase. Use the examples as guides to come up with challenges that will help you gradually move from what you are currently doing to what you want to be able to do.

Then, start climbing.

You are going to feel nervous. That's okay.

Actually, feeling nervous is good.

HOORay!

AWESOME!

Good for you!

Congratulations!

Way to go!

Well done!

BRAVO!

Right on!

Good on you!

It means you are on your way.

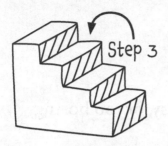

Step 3

3. Keep climbing.

Move along your staircase one step at a time. Make sure each step is a little harder than the one before.

Get something one aisle away

Get something from the end of the aisle with my parent at the opposite end

Get something off a shelf halfway down the aisle while my parent stays at the end

Walk several steps ahead of my parent

Stay right by my parent in the grocery store

Climbing might not be fun.

It might seem too hard, or too easy, or too boring.

You might be tempted to stop, or to get off your staircase entirely.

Don't give up.

If a challenge feels too hard, make it easier.

Parent stays in car for drop off

Parent stays outside at drop off

Parent walks me into school.
We say goodbye in the entry

Parent walks me part of the way to my
classroom. We say goodbye a few doors away

~~Parent walks me to my classroom and
says goodbye at the door~~ *Too hard!*

Parent walks me to my classroom and
comes in while I put my stuff away

Parent walks me to my classroom and stays in the doorway
while I put my stuff away. After a few days, parent
walks me to my classroom and says goodbye at the door

If the challenge you are working on feels too easy, make it harder by skipping ahead.

Finish the staircase, and do a yay-me dance. You did it! You climbed a staircase!

Some children find stair climbing boring. ho hum.

That's okay because in real life, stairs exist to get you someplace. They serve a purpose.

It's the same with these stairs. They get you somewhere.

Climbing re-trains your amygdala, which will make it easier to do the things you want and need to do.

That's not to say that every challenge has to be boring.

Use your imagination to spice things up.

Create games like:

Hide the Plate

Ask your parent to hide a plate (or some other item) in a room you usually avoid. Then, go find it on your own. Your parent can choose easy hiding places to begin with, and harder spots as you get more used to going to that room alone.

When you are going to school (or some other activity) on your own, you and your parent can come up with a list of things for you to find while you are there. Your list might include:

School Scavenger Hunt

- ☐ Someone wearing a red shirt.
- ☐ Someone with mismatched socks.
- ☐ Someone without any hair.
- ☐ Someone eating something that smells good.
- ☐ Someone with dog or cat hair on their clothing.
- ☐ Someone with a backpack you like.

Games make stair climbing more interesting and fun.

Rewards do, too.

Give yourself a point every time you do a challenge without complaining. When you get to 10 points, perhaps your parent will play a game with you, or do one of your chores, or let you have a backwards meal, with dessert first.

It also helps to remember why you are doing this. All the things that will be easier once you no longer have this fear.

Finally, keep in mind that separating from parents is something all animals do.

It's natural and part of life.

Hamsters do it. Horses do it. Hummingbirds do it. And you can do it, too.

Doing your steps every day will help you have fewer false alarms.

1. Quiet your brain.
2. Do the opposite.
3. Keep climbing.

You'll feel stronger, and braver, and happier.

And then you can get on with your life.

Note to Parents and Caregivers

The young of virtually all species look to their parents for protection. Humans are no exception. When they were little, your children not only wanted your presence—they needed it. Apprehension about being apart from parents is developmentally appropriate for little ones, and so ubiquitous that separation anxiety is considered *normal* for children prior to age 3. After that, it's a different story.

In most of the developed world, children are expected to attend school by age 5 or 6. Many go to preschool or daycare before that. For all sorts of reasons, we want and need our children to spend time apart from us, whether playing in a different part of the house or going to an activity on their own.

For some children, separation happens relatively smoothly. For others, even small bits of time apart is hard. They need company in the bathroom, and in their beds at night. They cling and cry and need repeated reassurance, even when they are clearly safe, even at activities they enjoy, or would enjoy, if anxiety wasn't swallowing them whole.

Children who have trouble separating from their parents (sometimes it is both parents, sometimes just one) often feel a sense of dread. They worry something will happen to their parent, or to them.

They worry that they'll need their parent, and that their parent will fail to materialize, this despite ample evidence to the contrary.

Occasionally, separation anxiety begins after an unfortunate experience, like getting stuck in a public bathroom or having a parent arrive slightly late for pick-up. But more typically, it begins without apparent reason, perhaps related to normal feelings of uncertainty and apprehension relieved by keeping a parent near. And then children begin to crave this comfort, to insist on it, feeling like they can't manage any uncertainty at all.

It's easy to fall into the habit of complying with an anxious child's apparent need. We don't want them to feel nervous, or uncomfortable. We want them to know that we'll be there for them, always. But this ever-availability turns out to be problematic. Our children get hooked on it, and it keeps them from learning how to trust other people, and trust themselves, and venture out into the world.

Facing Mighty Fears About Being Apart From Parents is for children ages 6–10 who have trouble navigating routine separations. It is not meant for children facing long-term separation from a parent due to illness, military deployment, work, or safety concerns. Nor is it meant for children whose parents are divorcing, or who are fearful of something it makes sense to be afraid of, like bullying at school. Sometimes separation fears occur alongside other fears, like the fear of "baddies," or animals, or throwing up. Parents of children with multiple fears might seek guidance from multiple sources including other books in the *Dr. Dawn's Mini Books About Mighty Fears* series and, if warranted, therapy.

Children will benefit most from reading this book with a supportive adult, preferably the parent they are having trouble separating from. It can be read all at once, or a section at a time. Either way, be sure to pause for the Fun Facts which not only entertain but also underline one of the main takeaways: that being apart from parents is common, and normal, and necessary, and fun. And that it's do-able.

Some additional tips

1. Children pick up on cues from the adults around them. Are they safe? Can they manage what is expected of them? When your child is in an anxious spiral, what they need—more than the rescue they seek—is an air of safety and calm. Learn to give that to your child. Breathe. Tell yourself, "My child is afraid, but they aren't in danger." Remain kind but firm. Your child can handle the challenge, whatever it is. You will help them.

2. Keep challenges small. Your child might not be able to manage a full school day without you, but they can handle 20 minutes. And then 40 minutes. And then an hour. They might not be able to go to an after-school activity alone, but they can learn to tolerate having you wait in another room, and then in the car. Think in terms of a staircase, with whatever you want your child to do at the top. What would be the equivalent of a single step toward that goal? Don't wait for situations to occur naturally. Instead, make a point of engineering mini separations. Small, frequent, intentional practice is the only way to turn this around.

3. Never sneak away from your child. It might be tempting to absorb your child in electronics so you can slip out, or to wait until they are happily engaged to call out a quick, "Bye," and

leave. Don't do that. Your child will be left with the disquieting notion that you can and will disappear at any time, causing them to become *more* vigilant. Even when good-byes are painful, it is essential that you give your child notice, and leave with their full awareness. Without that, they cannot trust you, and separation will remain problematic.

4. Anxious children have trouble tolerating uncertainty, even though life is full of it. Will you be there on time for pick-up? You'll certainly try. But you cannot guarantee that you will be first in line. The more your child pushes for promises, the more you need to remind them that this is a form of worry, and that "feeding" worry makes it grow. We do things that are *safe enough*, knowing that if a problem arises, we'll handle it, and there will be people there to help us. Your child doesn't need certainty. They need courage. You can help them develop that.

5. Reassurance-seeking is closely tied to the wish for certainty, and equally problematic. Children who struggle with separation get into the habit of asking lots of questions: Where are you going? How far is that? How long will you be gone? When will you be back? What if X or Y happens? And on and on. It's fine to tell your child the broad outlines of where you will be and what you will be doing, but it is counterproductive to go over and over the details, or to provide repeated reassurance that all will be well. Help your child learn to recognize, "That's Worry talking." Use the skills described in this book and other self-help materials (see the Resources section after this Note) to move away from providing endless reassurance.

6. It's okay for your child to feel nervous. It's okay for them to feel unsure. Uncomfortable feelings are part of life. Your goal is not to banish anxiety; it's to help your child learn to manage it. Managing anxiety means learning to face it, to move through it rather than away from it. The steps outlined in *Facing Mighty Fears About Being Apart From Parents* can help.

You can do this. Your child can do this. I'll be rooting for you.

Dr. Dawn

Resources

Organizations

These organizations provide information about childhood anxiety, and include therapist locators to assist with finding specialized care:

USA

The Anxiety and Depression Association of America: https://adaa.org

The International OCD Foundation: https://iocdf.org

UK

Anxiety UK: www.anxietyuk.org.uk

Young Minds: https://youngminds.org.uk

AU/NZ

Beyond Blue:
www.beyondblue.org.au

Kids Health:
https://kidshealth.org.nz

Please also reach out to your child's pediatrician for names of local providers.

Web-based resources

https://library.jkp.com
Dr. Dawn's Seven-Step Solution for When Worry Takes Over: Easy-to-Implement Strategies for Parents or Carers of Anxious Kids, see page 78.
Video Training Course

www.anxioustoddlers.com
Natasha Daniels of AT Parenting Survival creates podcasts, blog posts, and free resources about anxiety. She also offers subscription courses, coaching, and treatment.

https://childmind.org
This NY Institute offers articles on a host of topics, including anxiety, with a unique "Ask an Expert" feature providing trustworthy, relatable advice.

https://copingskillsforkids.com
Janine Halloran provides free, easy-to-implement, child-friendly tips on calming anxiety, managing stress, and more.

https://gozen.com
Kid-tested, therapist-approved, highly effective animated videos teaching skills related to anxiety, resilience, emotional intelligence, and more.

www.worrywisekids.org
Tamar Chansky of WorryWiseKids provides a treasure-trove of information for parents of anxious children.

Recommended reading

The books listed here are Dr. Dawn's current favorites, a snapshot from a particular moment in time. Please also search on your own, or check with your preferred bookseller, who can guide you toward up-to-date, appealing, effective books particularly suited to you and your child.

For younger children

Anxiety Relief Workbook for Kids: 40 Mindfulness, CBT, and ACT Activities to Find Peace from Anxiety and Worry by Agnes Selinger, PhD, Rockridge Press.

Hey Warrior: A Book for Kids about Anxiety by Karen Young, Little Steps Publishing.

Little Meerkat's Big Panic: A Story About Learning New Ways to Feel Calm by Jane Evans, Jessica Kingsley Publishers.

The Nervous Knight: A Story About Overcoming Worries and Anxiety by Anthony Lloyd Jones, Jessica Kingsley Publishers.

What to Do When You Worry Too Much: A Kid's Guide to Overcoming Anxiety by Dawn Huebner, PhD, American Psychological Association.

When Harley Has Anxiety: A Fun CBT Skills Activity Book to Help Manage Worries and Fears by Regine Galanti, PhD, Z Kids Publishing.

For older children

Coping Skills for Kids: Over 75 Coping Strategies to Help Kids Deal with Stress, Anxiety and Anger by Janine Halloran, PESI Publishing and Media.

Help! I've Got an Alarm Bell Going Off in My Head! How Panic, Anxiety and Stress Affect Your Body by K.L. Aspden, Jessica Kingsley Publishers.

My Anxiety Handbook by Sue Knowles, Bridie Gallagher, and Phoebe McEwen, Jessica Kingsley Publishers.

Name and Tame Your Anxiety: A Kid's Guide by Summer Batte, Free Spirit Publishing.

Outsmarting Worry: An Older Kid's Guide to Managing Anxiety by Dawn Huebner, PhD, Jessica Kingsley Publishers.

Superpowered: Transform Anxiety into Courage, Confidence, and Resilience by Renee Jain and Shefali Tsabary, PhD, Random House Books for Young Readers.

Take Control of OCD: A Kid's Guide to Conquering Anxiety and Managing OCD, 2nd Edition by Bonnie Zucker, PsyD, Routledge Press.

For parents

Anxious Kids, Anxious Parents: 7 Ways to Stop the Worry Cycle and Raise Courageous and Independent Children by Reid Wilson, PhD, and Lynn Lyons, LICSW, Health Communications Inc.

Breaking Free of Child Anxiety and OCD: A Scientifically Proven Program for Parents by Eli R. Lebowitz, PhD, Oxford University Press.

Freeing Your Child from Anxiety, Revised and Updated Edition: Practical Strategies to Overcome Fears, Worries, and Phobias and Be Prepared for Life by Tamar Chansky, PhD, Harmony.

Growing Up Mindful: Essential Practices to Help Children, Teens and Families Find Balance, Calm, and Resilience by Christopher Willard, PsyD, Sounds True.

Peaceful Parent, Happy Kids: How to Stop Yelling and Start Connecting by Laura Markham, PhD, TarcherPerigee.

The No Worries Guide to Raising Your Anxious Child: A Handbook to Help You and Your Anxious Child Thrive by Karen Lynn Cassiday, PhD, Jessica Kingsley Publishers.

The Yes Brain: How to Cultivate Courage, Curiosity and Resilience in Your Child by Dan Siegel, MD, and Tina Payne Bryson, PhD, Bantam Press.

Dr. Dawn's
SEVEN-STEP SOLUTION
FOR WHEN WORRY TAKES OVER
Easy-to-Implement Strategies for
Parents or Carers of Anxious Kids

worry has a way of turning into WORRY in the blink of an eye. This upper-case WORRY causes children to fret about unlikely scenarios and shrink away from routine challenges, ultimately holding entire families hostage. But upper-case WORRY is predictable and manageable once you understand its tricks.

This 7-video series will help you recognize WORRY's tricks while teaching a handful of techniques to help you and your child break free.

Each video contains learning objectives and action steps along with need-to-know content presented in a clear, engaging manner by child psychologist and best-selling author, Dr. Dawn Huebner. The videos are available from https://library.jkp.com.

Video One: Trolling for Danger (time 8:15)

- The role of the amygdala in spotting and alerting us to danger
- What happens when the amygdala sets off an alarm
- Real dangers versus false alarms
- Calming the brain (yours and your child's) to get back to thinking

Video Two: The Worry Loop (time 10:15)

- The "loop" that keeps Worry in place
- How to identify where your child is in the Worry Loop

Video Three: Externalizing Anxiety (time 11:41)

- Externalizing anxiety as a powerful first step
- Talking back to Worry
- Teaching your child to talk back to Worry
- Talking back without entering into a debate

Video Four: Calming the Brain and Body (time 13:36)

- Breathing techniques
- Mindfulness techniques
- Distraction techniques
- Which technique (how to choose)?

Video Five: Getting Rid of Safety Behaviors (time 15:18)

- Preparation
- The role of exposure
- Explaining exposure to your child
- Creating an exposure hierarchy

Video Six: Worrying Less Is Not the Goal (time 13:02)

- The more you fight anxiety, the more it holds on
- The more you accommodate anxiety, the more it stays
- Anxiety is an error message, a false alarm
- When you stop letting Worry be in charge, it fades

Video Seven: Putting It All Together (time 19:42)

- A review of the main techniques
- Deciding where to start
- The role of rewards
- Supporting your child, not Worry